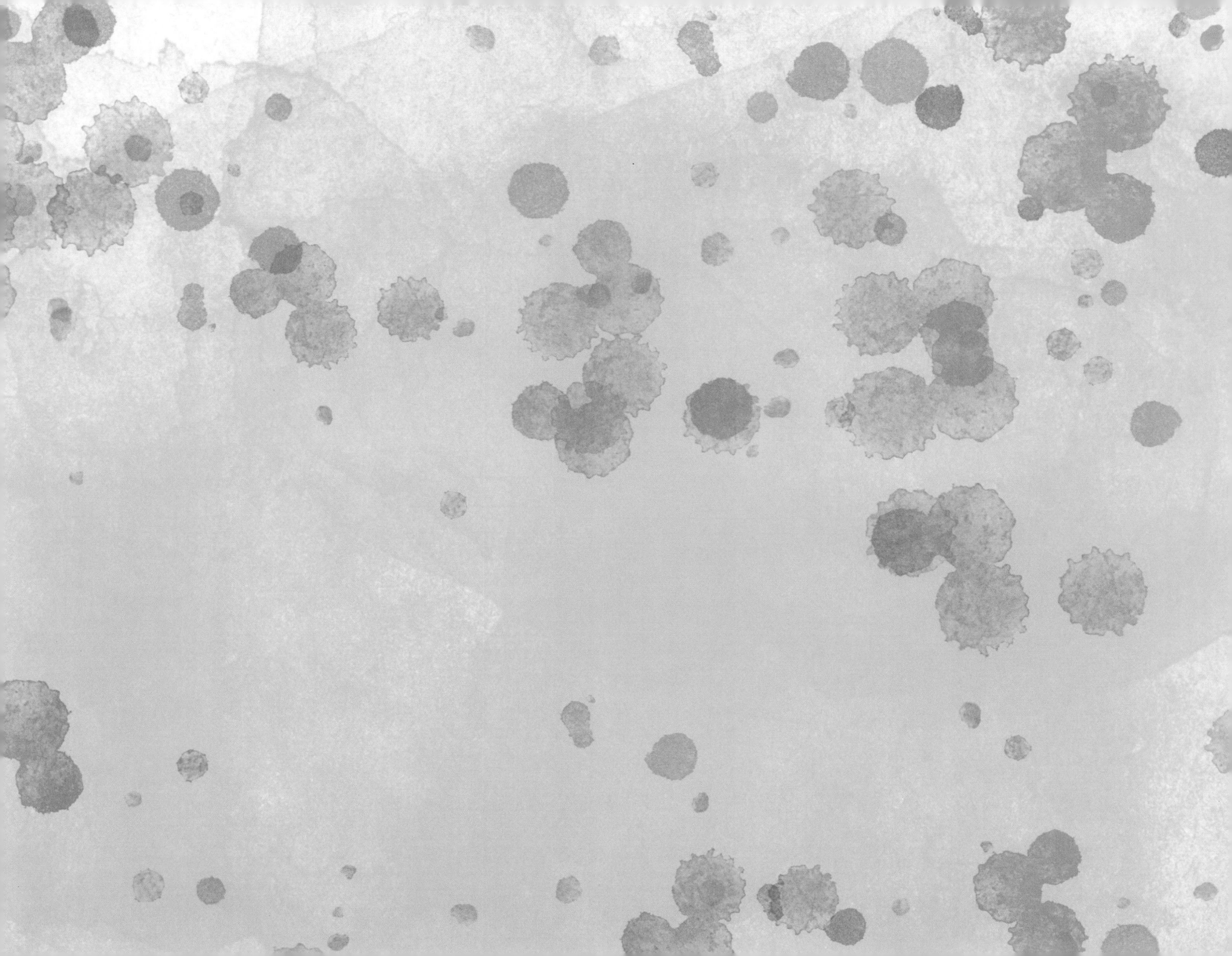

Elementary Teachers: This One is For You

©2025 Jim Addison

Illustrations by Tania Tokar

ISBN: 979-8-9930942-0-5

All Rights Reserved

To the teacher who unlocks the classroom door before the world awakes. You may not realize it, but you are about to change someone's life today.

Marcus pulls on his shoes with frayed laces. His little brother clings to his leg. Mom's already at job number two. Eight years old. Already carrying more than he should.

To the teacher who knows that sometimes showing up is an act of bravery, thank you for greeting every child with grace.

At school, Marcus slumps in his chair.
He misses his dad. Newly deployed. Silent.
A crumpled photo buried in his desk.
He doesn't speak, but his silence is loud.

To the teacher who kneels beside the desk
and says, "I'm glad you're here."
You are the reason some kids
begin to believe they matter.

It's time to practice decoding words.
Marcus avoids eye contact.
The concept just isn't sticking,
But you don't give up.

To the teacher who whispers, "Let's try it together," and who celebrates effort louder than perfection. You are rewriting stories every single day.

Recess.
Marcus watches from the edge of the blacktop.
You encourage. Invite. Laugh.
He joins the game.

To the teacher who knows that connection comes before curriculum, you are building more than just academic growth.
You are building trust.

In the afternoon,
Marcus finally raises his hand.

It's a small question.

But it's big
for him.

And you light up like
it's the best question
in the world.

To the teacher who notices every small win, thank you for holding up a mirror when students forget their brilliance.

The fire alarm blares.
Marcus panics.
You crouch beside him.
Voice calm. Hand steady.
You walk slowly, together.

Dismissal.
Marcus lingers.
"Will you be here tomorrow?" he asks.
You smile. "Of course."

To the teacher who shows up again and again.

Even when the work is heavy,
Even when the wins are quiet,
Even when no one is watching.

The work you do is not always seen.
Not always appreciated. Understood.
But it echoes in the lives of your students.

So, whether it is the start of
a new year.
A new week.
A new chapter.

Remember that you are not just educating your students.

You are selflessly giving them a piece of yourself.
Your passion. Kindness. Knowledge. Love.

You may never know
the full impact you are making.
But to Marcus and so many others,
you are unforgettable.

There will be hard days.
There will be long nights.
But there will also be small miracles,
and you will be at the center of them.

So on the days when it all feels heavy, when the lesson flops, the copier jams, or no one thinks to say thank you, please read this book again.

For all that you do
For all that you are.
And for all the lives you touch.
One quiet, powerful day at a time.

Because Teachers, this one is for you.

www.ingramcontent.com/pod-product-compliance
Lightning Source LLC
Chambersburg PA
CBRC102257090526
44582CB00016B/195